Xiron Poetry Club

磨 铁 读 诗 会

维马丁诗选

SELECTED POEMS BY MARTIN WINTER

最终我们赢得了雪

FINALLY WE HAVE SNOW

[奥地利] 维马丁 著 伊沙 老G 译

四川文艺出版社

目录

自序

文 | 维马丁

自己的诗歌被中国大诗人伊沙翻译成中文，在世界上人口最多的国度中国出版，被著名诗人沈浩波创办的磨铁图书公司选中，应该写篇什么样的自序表达心情呢？

我最关心的东西总是诗歌本身，特别是中国当代诗歌，用汉语普通话写作的诗歌。当然中国还有很多其他非常好的东西，包括用汉语之外的语言写的或唱的作品，用中国少数民族语言或方言创作的作品，等等。某种意义上来说，我自己知道并深感荣幸的是，我可以参与一些文学方面的事或活动。那么在当下文学的世界里，有多少人关注的是文学之外的事情呢？非常多，我要说，这种情况在中国和其他各国都很普遍。

中国到底是怎么样的？为什么要问这个问题？其实很多人都会这样问，包括很多中国人自己。因为中国很大，而且中国目前在全球经济中扮演重要角色，所以全世界各地的人都会这样问。同样的问题，奥地利是怎么样的？美国呢？拉脱维亚呢？巴西呢？这两三年在全世界范围内，难民问题、就业问题、种族问题等等，很多情况一直每况愈下。与此同时，无论在哪里，关注自然环境问题的人都越来越多；还有一种感觉是，人们意识到对抗是必须的，用于反对某些不好的趋势。所以也许可以说，我们还有希望。

那么这些问题跟伊沙翻译我的诗歌有什么直接关系吗？也许有，也许没有。伊沙说他一直觉得应该关注中国或东亚之外的西方当代诗歌，从他开始写作起就一直这样想。我也一直这样觉得，要关注外国的诗歌。生活在奥地利，这个情况对我来说也许更复杂一些，比如我上大学时，虽然除了汉学也攻读了德语文学，我自己当然也用当代德语写作，但是德语文学不是我主要关注的。这样的背景和态度当然有长处也有短处。

总之，我走进了当代汉语诗歌，这很像一个奇迹。从 2013 年我第一次跟伊沙见面，我一直觉得伊沙就是在创造奇迹，伊沙创造和组织了一个奇迹般的诗歌疆域——《新世纪诗典》，比我以往在其他任何地方碰到的文学组织都要开放，比我以往见到的文学形态都更接近普通人和真实的生活。所以我更觉得非常非常荣幸，非常非常幸福。中国对我来说，是一个以西安和诗歌为中心的奇迹，是古老的西安和古代中国的诗歌传统延续至今天的奇迹。

2019 年春天于维也纳

PREFACE

by Martin Winter

When your poetry gets translated into Chinese by the world-famous poet Yi Sha and published in the most populous country on earth by the world-famous poet Shen Haobo and his publishing company, what do you say?

Poetry is what I want to talk about all the time. Chinese poetry, most often. Of course there are so many other great things, including what people write or sing in other languages, or in different kinds of Chinese. But what I understand, to some degree, and feel very honored to participate in is literature, basically. And in today's literature, how many people are there who care about things outside of literature? I would say there are many, maybe a majority, in China and also in other places.

What exactly is China like? Why do you ask? Actually, many people are asking such questions. Many Chinese, also all sorts of people all over. Because China is very big and has a big role in global economics right now. What is Austria like? America? Latvia? Brazil? In the past two years, many places over the world had become worse in terms of solidarity, for workers, for ordinary people, for helping each other. At the same time, awareness for environment issues has generally increased. And there is a feeling that resistance is needed, against some trends. So there is hope, you could say.

What does this have to do with Yi Sha translating my poems? Well, maybe poetry is directly related to such issues. Or maybe not. Yi Sha said he always felt he should be following current poetry abroad, ever since he grew up and started writing. Me too, I thought the same. Living in Austria, maybe I am a little more radical, because although I had two majors, both Chinese studies and German language and literature, and although I am participating in German-language literature, this current German-language literature is not my focus. And this kind of background and attitude obviously has positive and negative consequences.

Anyway, how did I get here? It feels like a miracle. From 2013, when I first met Yi Sha, even before, watching his *NPC* unfolding online, and starting to participate; I knew he was working miracles. Writing, translating, teaching and editing, he was creating a land more open and generous than anything I had ever encountered in any language. This is a land in literature, but very close to life, to people whose life isn't about literature, not consciously. So I feel very honored, very lucky and very happy. To me China is a miracle coming out of Xi'an, the ancient magical city, located in today's center of avant-garde poetry.

Spring 2019, Vienna

世界

世界变空变冷。

心中有房

继而下雪。

外面有暴风雪

北京一片白色；

实际上他们早在十一月便为城市供暖，

雪一直下着

这很确定。

柳树的叶子仍然未落

所以它们被击倒了，还有其他很多树。

这是一个美好的冬日

人们对外国宝宝很友好。

一周前

我们去了地坛公园

玛雅玩银杏叶

还有五颜六色的大叶子。

我们谈到王朝的

衰落与灭亡。

不安全感。

以及如何证明自己，然后我们回家
在路上吃了小笼包穿过
大楼小巷的迷宫。
喜鹊们喜欢待在树叶中间，
我想它们暂时可以
安度整个冬天。
感觉像在下雪
闻起来就像我小时候在阿尔卑斯山某处度假时的冬天
虽然是在下雨
就在几天前，在雨下了一个月后，我感觉自己站在屋顶上
少有干燥的时候，这一年是湿的。
我们祝你们大家冬天快乐
我们可以快乐地欢聚
在不久后的某一天重逢。
太阳出来了，我们和玛雅一起
去看雪中的玫瑰
星期天礼拜，听音乐
吃比萨和沙拉，然后打个盹儿
在自行车上或在楼上，
虽然她现在终于安静下来，但比起往常还是不够安静。
我们在沿街小店里给她买了一双温暖舒适的鞋子，
她穿着凉鞋和滑雪服，骑着自行车出去了。

她的屁股正在痊愈，她脸颊上有斑点，
她长了十颗牙，一个大孩子喜欢她，
一个看起来像四岁的姐姐，
比别的孩子大一半的样子
声音像她父亲。玛雅，她说，玛雅，
我们应该像妈妈或爸爸那样站一会儿。
我应该写完
一本书再写另一本书，还要喝点茶。

2003

THE WORLD

the world is getting empty and cold.
there is room for the mind
and then there is snow.
there is a thunderstorm outside
and beijing is white;
and they are actually heating the city in early november,
and the snow stays on
just to make sure.
the willows still had all their leaves
and so they broke down, and many other trees.
it is a wonderful winter day
and people are nice to foreign babies.
one week ago
we went to the park round the earth altar
and maia played with the ginkgo leaves
and bigger ones in many colours.
we talked about falls
of dynasties and decay.
and not feeling safe.

and proving yourself, and then we went home
and ate xiaolongbao on the way through the maze
of little lanes and lots of construction.
the magpies liked it among the leaves,
i guess they'll be fine
throughout the winter for a while.
it felt like snow
and smelled like in winter when i was a child in the holidays in a place in the alps
although it was rain
just a few days ago that i felt on the roof after it fell after a month or less of dryness, the year was wet.
we wish you all a merry winter
and may we be happy together
again some day soon.
the sun is out; we went with maia
to see the roses in the snow
and sunday service, and listen to music
and pizza and salad and then dozing off
on the bicycle and also upstairs,
but not quite enough as it always happens although at last she is quiet now.

we bought her shoes which are warm and comfy in a little store
along the way,
after leading her out on the bike in her sandals and a skiing suit.
her butt is healing, her cheeks have spots,
she has ten teeth, the big one likes her,
the older sister who looks like four,
is one and a half other children's size
and sounds like her father. maia, said she, maia,
as often as mama or papa when we had staid for a while.
i should be working
to finish a book and start on another and drink some tea.

2003

没啥好说的

没啥好说的
到处都是建筑工人
拆除和重建
没啥好说的
他们是满载歌声的孩子
踏着欧罗巴进行曲
大呼小叫，上下挥舞
没啥好说的
他们踢踏秋天的落叶
他们惊飞成群的鸟儿
今年提前降临的温暖
在城市的散热器中
没啥好说的
他们卖杂货
和欧洲车
全都装饰幽暗的窗子
践踏小卷心菜叶子
它们被非法销售
没啥好说的

它们是古老的护城河

人人保持健康

他们勉强过活

他们站在街上

他们卖 vcd

没啥好说的

一切都能买到

毕竟，这儿是北京

2004

THERE IS NOTHING TO DESCRIBE

there is nothing to describe
they are all construction workers
tearing down and building up
there is nothing to describe
they are children full of songs
european marching tunes
shouting, waving up and down
there is nothing to describe
they are dancing autumn leaves
they are soaring flocks of birds
there is early heat this year
in the city's radiators
there is nothing to describe
they are selling groceries
and the european car
all decked out in darkened windows
tramples little cabbage leaves
they are sold illegally
there is nothing to describe

they are ancient city moats
everybody keeping fit
they are trying to get by
they are standing on the street
they are selling vcd
there is nothing to describe
there is everything to buy
this is beijing, after all

2004

下辈子

下辈子我是一块石头
下辈子你会成为什么
你死的时候会变作什么
这个问题问得并不准确
下辈子没有世界
我们累了，它便在此
在这早晨，上帝希望
我是一张纸，下辈子
下辈子我是一个孩子
下辈子你会成为什么
你死的时候会变作什么
这个问题问得并不准确
下辈子没有世界
它与我们同在，当我们在此
在这早晨，上帝希望
我的孩子在此，这辈子

2007.8

NEXT TIME AROUND

i am a rock next time around
what will you be in your next life
what will you be when you are dead
the question is not accurate
there is no world next time around
when we are tired, it is here
and in the morning, god be willing
i'm paper then next time around
next time around i am a child
what will you be in your next life
what will you be when you are dead
the question is not accurate
there is no world next time around
it is with us, when we are there
and in the morning, god be willing
my child is here this time around

August 2007

一无所有

没啥好说的
我们是平头百姓
对盖了又拆
没啥好说的

没啥好解释的
我们是平头百姓
对盖了又拆
没啥好解释的

没啥好记住的
我们是平头百姓
对盖了又拆
没啥好记住的

没啥好期待的
我们是平头百姓
对盖了又拆
没啥好期待的

没啥好遗憾的
我们是平头百姓
对盖了又拆
没啥好遗憾的

没啥好忘记的
我们是平头百姓
对盖了又拆
没啥好忘记的

2007.8

THERE IS NOTHING

there is nothing to describe
we are ordinary people
building up and tearing down
there is nothing to describe

there is nothing to explain
we are ordinary people
building up and tearing down
there is nothing to explain

there is nothing to remember
we are ordinary people
building up and tearing down
there is nothing to remember

there is nothing to expect
we are ordinary people
building up and tearing down
there is nothing to expect

there is nothing to regret
we are ordinary people
building up and tearing down
there is nothing to regret

there is nothing to forget
we are ordinary people
building up and tearing down
there is nothing to forget

August 2007

九月的早晨

我在晨曦中吻你
耳听清晨群鸟的啼鸣
目睹爬山虎爬上屋顶
一场渴望中的雨终于未下
但天已凉了
而你是暖的

2007.9

SEPTEMBER MORNING

i kiss you in the morning light

i hear the morning sounds of birds

i see the flowers on the roof

it should have rained a while ago

but it is cool

and you are warm

September 2007

月亮

今夜格外月圆

不知你在何方

我们坐在楼下吃零食

空气清新，一点儿都不冷

但你能感觉到正在凝结的白霜

五点以后天很快就黑了

站起来，往家走。

2007.10

THE MOON

the moon is round again tonight
and so i wonder where you are
we sit and eat some snacks downstairs
the air is balmy, not yet cold
but you can feel the coming frost
and it gets dark soon after five
so please get up and let's go home.

October 2007

小儿

小儿起夜起床玩
我们大于我们的存在
有时我们可以称之为上帝
一到十二点便哭闹
有时我们可以称之为光明
一到两点钟便哭闹
总是在夜里哭闹

小儿起夜醒来哭
我们少于我们的存在
一到中午便睡觉
有时我们可以称之为上帝
一过八点钟便哭闹
有时我们可以看到光明
小儿随时吵闹我们
有时我们能感受夜晚
有时小家伙完美无缺

2007.10

LITTLE WEE

little wee gets up to play
we are more than what we are
sometimes we may call it god
wee may call as soon as twelve
sometimes we may call it light
wee may call as soon as two
wee may always call at night

little wee wakes up to cry
we are less than what we are
wee may sleep as soon as noon
sometimes we may call it god
wee may call as late as eight
sometimes we can see the light
wee can call us any time
sometimes we can feel the night
sometimes wee can be alright

October 2007

我父亲的手

我父亲的手
不像我的
他的手很大
在我儿时
他的手很硬
他盖了一幢房子
他的手很温暖
现在仍然很大
我父亲的手
他个子不高
也许他的手
并没有那么大
我儿子很小
他的手很软
会像我的手吗
我们拭目以待

2008.3

MY FATHER'S HANDS

my father's hands
are not like mine
his hands were big
when i was small
his hands were hard
he built a house
his hands were warm
they are still big
my father's hands
he is not tall
maybe his hands
are not that big
my son is small
his hands are soft
are they like mine
we'll wait and see

March 2008

群星

星星那么遥远
城市臭气熏天
但这还真不算太糟糕
让我们去睡觉

2008.4

THE STARS

the stars are far

the city stinks

but it's really not too bad

let's go to sleep

April 2008

祈祷

祈祷旗帜飘扬
这儿只是一座幼儿园
小旗迎风飘扬
条条道路穿过院落
祈祷旗帜飘扬
那是今天的风

2008.4

PRAYER

prayer flags are fluttering
it is just a kindergarten
little flags are fluttering
all the way across the yard
prayer flags are fluttering
it is just the wind today

April 2008

欲飞谣

今宵月儿又重圆
昨夜它又圆又大
今宵月儿又重圆
明朝你将欲飞去

今宵月儿又重圆
月儿躲在高楼后
今宵月儿又重圆
明朝你将欲飞去

夜凉散发鱼腥臭
今宵月儿又重圆
夜凉溢出茉莉香
下月我们要远行

2008.5

FLY

the moon is round again today
the moon was round and great last night
the moon is round again today
tomorrow you will fly away

the moon is round again today
the moon is right behind the house
the moon was great and round last night
tomorrow you will fly away

the night is cool and reeks of fish
the moon is round again today
the night is cool with jasmine scent
next month we're going far away

May 2008

玫瑰

——写于四川地震后

一年中最美好的时光
当所有玫瑰全都开放
好雨知时节
大气亦清新

一年中最美好的时光
飓风和地震接踵而至
还有先前所有的一切
当春乃发生

2008.5

ROSES

—after the sichuan earthquake

it is the best time of the year
when all the roses are in bloom
this year the rain was very good
and so the air is not too bad

it is the best time of the year
a cyclone and an earthquake too
and everything that went before
it is the best time of the year

May 2008

说话

说话很廉价
歌声是憧憬
与悲痛
孩子们唱歌
孩子们跳舞
孩子们说话
孩子们活蹦乱跳
说话被留下
说话是对的
说话很廉价
日复一日

2008.6

TALK

talk is cheap

song is lon-

ging and grief

children sing

children dance

children talk

children prance

talk is left

talk is right

talk is cheap

day and night

June 2008

此地

昨晚你看见月亮了吗
不，我不曾看见月亮
前天晚上呢
有一阵子没见到它了
刚好在我们离开前就看到了
在夜半
我们到达的那夜也看到过
我们在雷雨中飞行
看见云层上方光芒万丈
甚至看到一两颗星星
就在我们睡着之前
现在我累了
我很高兴来到此地

2008.7

HERE

did you see the moon last night

no, i didn't see the moon

what about the night before

haven't seen it for a while

saw it right before we left

in the middle of the night

saw the night when we arrived

we flew through a thunderstorm

saw the light above the clouds

even saw a star or two

right before we fell asleep

i am tired even now

i am happy to be here

July 2008

空气

空气凉爽
蟋蟀歌唱
我猜就在对街某个地方
我不知道我是否能看见星星
我从这里从未看见过月亮

空气凉爽，我睡不着
在夜里，空气寂静
在早晨，群鸟齐鸣

2008.7

AIR

the air is cool

the crickets sing

somewhere across the street i guess

i don't know if i've seen a star

i never see the moon from here

the air is cool and i can't sleep

and in the night the air is still

and in the morning there are birds

July 2008

望月

昨晚你看见月亮了吗
它在此处，在林间
它升起来，在东山
在大地之上
在多瑙河大桥上
在我们家后院的一棵树中
在与友共进晚餐后
昨晚你看见月亮了吗
对你来说它意味着什么
当你看到月圆之时
你有过在家里的感觉吗
它让你想起朋友
想起你留在身后的一切吗
昨晚很冷
一年前我们从北京的阳台上望月
猜想明年我们会在这里看到它
昨晚你看见月亮了吗
我们正在两地之间

2008.9

SEE THE MOON

did you see the moon last night
it was here between the trees
it was up there in the sky
up above the underground
up above the danube bridge
in a tree in our backyard
after dinner with some friends
did you see the moon last night
did it mean something to you
did you ever feel at home
when you saw the moon was full
did it make you think of friends
think of what you left behind
it was rather cold last night
we saw the moon a year ago
from our balcony in beijing
guess we'll see it here next year
did you see the moon last night
we are somewhere in between

September 2008

盒子

我们收到一大堆书
还有家具和陶器
我们终于拥有了自己的床
还有很多我已忘记的东西
你说它找回了你的生命
我们常年漂泊在外
睡在别人的床上
也许没有多到可怕
我们收到一大堆书
餐具和窗帘
我们也有很多争执
不管怎样，还行
与人为邻
慢慢来挺好的
我们收到很多东西
感觉就像昨天我们才离开
需要几年才能在这里安顿好

2008.10

BOXES

we have received a load of books
and furniture and crockery
and finally we have our bed
and lots of stuff that i forgot
you say it gave you back your life
we had a lot of life without
our bed in other people's beds
or maybe not an awful lot
we have received a load of books
and tableware and draperies
we also had a lot of strife
and anyway, it was ok
in other people's neighborhoods
it was ok to take it slow
we have received a lot of stuff
it feels like yesterday we left
it will take years to settle here

October 2008

朋友们

玛雅想和你们在一起
你们的照片挂满每个房间
她想打电话给你们
她拿着手机打起来
她说她有你们的电话
她想和陈泽洋在一起
她想和朱阿姨在一起
她想和她所有的朋友在一起
有时她在晚上为你们祈祷
晚上她睡觉前
让每个人都做个好梦
然后我们可以睡个通宵

2008.11

FRIENDS

maia wants to be with you
your pictures hang in every room
she wants to call you on the phone
she brings her phone and picks it up
she says she has you on the phone
she wants to be with chen zeyang
she wants to be with zhu ayi
she wants to be with all her friends
sometimes at night she prays for you
at night before she goes to sleep
let everybody have good dreams
and may we sleep the whole night through

November 2008

诗

诗是人
是人的错误
是缺少的话语
还有一些不是
一天是一首诗
一天是一头野兽
一步是一首诗
至少是我看到的海和光
一道裂缝是一首诗
诗是租金
一天中的眼泪
冷与风
但是谁拥有岁月
但是什么是脚步
野兽在何方
谁拥有房租
何为我所言
何为我们所悼
何为我所能
都遍寻不见

2008.11

POEMS

poems are people

are people mistaken

are words that are wanting

and some that are not

a day is a poem

a day is a beast

a step is a poem

the sea the light i see at least

a cleft is a poem

and poems are rents

a tear in the day

the cold and the wind

but who has the days

and what are the steps

and where are the beasts

and who has the rent

what is it i say

what is it we mourn

what is it i may

not find in the least

November 2008

祝词

月升月落
四海同此一月
在我们住处很难看到他
也许不那么难
我们以前有阳台
屋顶上的露台
只有六层楼高
屋顶在七楼
我走到户外，看到了月亮
你走到户外，感觉到空气
并非到处都是玫瑰
他们在院子里栽了一些玫瑰
我现在得出去看看
我得再去寻找他
你不知道他是否吃饱了
你不知道他是否变瘦了
云朵漂亮地飞奔
我不知道明年我们在何方

2009.3

GREETINGS

the moon has many ups and downs
the moon is everywhere the same
it's hard to see him where we live
or maybe it's not all that hard
we had a balcony before
a terrace high up on the roof
not all that high just six floors up
the roof was on the seventh floor
i stepped outside and saw the moon
you stepped outside and felt the air
it wasn't roses everywhere
they have some roses in the yard
i have to go out now and see
i have to look him up again
you don't know if he's getting full
you don't know if he's getting thin
the clouds are going pretty fast
i don't know where we'll be next year

March 2009

春天

雨水冲走了雪后
的污泥；感觉像春天
月亮快要满了
农历元月
二月最后两天
无论我们在这城里干什么
都几乎从未有过家的感觉
但无论如何月亮是大的
我们在一起并且活着

2010.2

SPRING

the rain has washed away the dirt
left from the snow; it feels like spring
the moon is going to be full
the first one of the lunar year
the last two days of february
what are we doing in this town
it hardly ever felt like home
but anyway the moon is big
we are together and alive

February 2010

维也纳

看见雕像如何坐落
在门庭之上，当你骑车经过时
看见灯火通明光芒四射
仿佛影子在有轨电车上穿过
透过车窗玻璃你可以穿越迷宫
当你长大，心便如斯
或者它像一本摊开的书
你正在骑行，你想说
你骑着你的自行车，当你凝视
有时会得到一派好风光
比昨天、前天都好
比更前一天也好
或者也许相反。你会看到更多
当你死时
也许你会坐着，仿佛你还活着

2010.3

VIENNA

to see the statues how they're sitting
above the gate when you ride by
to see the glowing lights transmitting
through window panes as shadows glide
a streetcar takes you through the maze
when you grew up your heart was like
or was it like an open book
you're riding on, you want to say
you ride your bike, and as you gaze
you sometimes get a better look
than yesterday, the day before
the day before another day
or maybe not. you'll look some more
and when you die
maybe you'll sit and seem alive

March 2010

威尼斯

一座开满鲜花的庭院的气息
正午太阳的一条通道
一幢房子，一片水域，整座城市
一千年变作一日
他们知道在这里，你很快就将死去
每个人都会来说
你可以要求什么，留下什么
然后他们做好离开的准备
因为我们在这个世界住过
我们做过什么，我们听到什么
一种气息，一块石头，一丝声响，一个计划
一份请求理解的抗辩

2010.6

VENICE

one yard of scents, with blossoms filled
one passage through the midday sun
one house, one water, one whole town
one thousand years become one day
they know it here, you'll die quite soon
and everyone will come and say
what you may claim, and what remains
and then they're ready to depart
'cause what we are stays in this world
what we have done, what we have heard
one scent, one stone, one sound, one plan
a plea that says please understand

June 2010

尤尔马拉

大海，海鸥，风吹雨打的大海
波浪，光，夜的波浪
海岸，沙滩，风吹雨打的沙滩
松树，虫子，蓝莓
又是光，鸟儿在飞翔
细看与谛听
嗅觉，气味，风和雨
松树，虫子，草莓
又是光，天空，夜

还有前几天的太阳
海滩上的每个人
祖父母，孩子，年轻人
你爬着玩，感觉到自在

2010.7

JURMALA

the sea, the gulls, the windswept sea
the waves, the light, the waves at night
the shore, the sand, the windswept sands
the pines, the bugs, the blueberries
again the light, the birds in flight
the seeing and the listening
the scents, the smells, the wind and rain
the pines, the bugs, the strawberries
again the light, the sky, the night

and then the sun the other day
and everybody on the beach
the grandparents, the kids, the youth
you crawl and play and feel alright

July 2010

亲近

靠近你的入口
靠近你的窗棂
靠近你的蜡烛
靠近你的耳朵

亲近日落
亲近行星
亲近沙洲
亲近尘土

就在水面以下
就在地毯下面
在运动之下亲近
在夜色之下亲近

亲近你的感情
亲近你的烦恼
亲近你的阳台
亲近你的屋顶

淹没屋顶

淹没水面
淹没身体
淹没你的皮肤

靠近你的水桶
靠近你的铲子
靠近你的猎枪
亲近你的爱情

人与人亲密无间
海龟和蟋蟀
蚂蚁和青蛙

越过群山
越过河流
越过树冠
亲近地球

亲近你的心跳
亲近你的肩膀
亲近你的呼吸
亲近你的嘴唇

2010.8

CLOSE

close to your entrance
close to your window
close to your candle
and close to your ear

close to the sunset
close to the planets
close to the sandbanks
close to the dust

just under the surface
just under the blanket
close under the movement
close under the night

close to your feelings
close to your worries
close to your balcony
close to your roof

close over the rooftops

close over the water

close over the bodies

close over your skin

close to your buckets

close to your shovels

close to your shotguns

close to your love

very close between the people

the turtles and the crickets

the ants and the frogs

and over the mountains

and over the rivers

and over the treetops

and close to the earth

close to your heartbeat

close to your shoulders

close to your breathing

and close to your mouth

August 2010

圣诞诗

你为什么不在明日的四月叫醒我
你为什么不让我和六月同在
十二月我能在这儿干什么
我真的不知道，我真的不在乎
谁在乎你说什么，谁知道你的感受
只要我醒来，便知道你在那里
只要我们工作，面包就摆放在桌上
只要孩子们长得健康强壮
让我继续干一年或者十年
甚至五十年。让我们一起醒来
向着对方醒来。向着孩子和朋友
向着父母和历史、亲戚、鲜花
只要我们能做到，我们就在这里生息
从始到终，循环往复，充满力量

2010.12

CHRISTMAS POEM

why don’t you wake me tomorrow in april
why don’t you put me together in june
what am i doing december here for
i really don’t know and i really don’t care
who cares what you say and who knows what you feel
as long as i wake up and know you are there
as long as we work and put bread on the table
as long as the children grow healthy and strong
just let me go on for a year or a decade
or even for fifty. let’t wake up together
wake up to each other. to children and friends
to parents and history, relatives, flowers
as long as we can we are here for a living
of many beginnings and powers and ends

December 2010

樱

闪烁、飘浮、洁白、粉红
被抬进今天
在疯狂的人丛之中
唯有这些树木常青
花开花谢
傲然屹立，吐纳风雨

2011.4

BLOSSOM

shine and float in white and pink

carried forth into the day

all among the loony people

certainly the trees are blooming

growing, falling, ripening

standing, breathing in the wind

April 2011

特热比奇

又干了
至少在路上
不再下雨
星期一在外面荡秋千
我们仍未爬上这座塔
还没见到那座古老的大教堂
他们只是偶尔让你进去
与捷克游客一起。那很好
但我们昨天很饿。

这是座很特别的城镇
关于犹太人的部分保存得很好
教堂很大。你应该进去
到地下。在祭坛
后面，粉刷过的十三世纪的墙壁
天花板。
圣普罗科普是监护人
征服火神、铁链与黑色。
一切在这里结束。他们也是这么说

《哈利·波特》的，3D版。
广场后面的小巷
与当地黑帮有染。
别担心，警察够多。

铁路桥，墓地
这座伤痕累累的老城周围的小山
走廊里的燕子
位于兹诺伊莫的旅行者旅馆
耶维绍维采的、
胡布克马维奇的墙，等等
维纳斯和陶器
值得到此一游，所有这一切。

2011.8

TŘEBÍČ

it's dry again
at least the road
it doesn't rain
and monday is in swing outside
we haven't climbed the tower yet
and haven't seen the old big church
they only let you in at times
with tourists in czech. that's quite ok
but we were hungry yesterday.

this is a very special town
the jewish side is well preserved
the church is big. you should go in
and underground. and in the back
behind the altar, painted walls
and ceiling, 13th century.
st. procop is the guardian
subdues a vulcan, chained and black.
it all ends here. that's what they say

for *harry potter*, in 3d.

the alleys right behind the square

have dramas with the local gangs.

don’t worry, there’s enough police.

the railway bridge, the cemetery

the hills around this scarred old town

the swallows in the corridors

the traveller’s inn, in znojmo too

the walls of jevišovice

hluboké mašůvky and such

the venus and the pottery

well worth a visit, everything.

August 2011

布尔诺：彼得与保罗大教堂

这光明，这天使加百利。

这夕光，这西方，这东方。

这火车，这从西边驶来的街车。

这城市的众塔林立。

我们不知道光明来自何方。

太阳升起，群星永恒。

我们沉睡，我们苏醒，

我们学习，我们教育，

我们生育，我们劳作。

我们不知道光明何时熄灭。

我们只知道太阳照常升起。

我们不知道光明来自何方。

2011.8

PETER AND PAUL CATHEDRAL, BRNO

the light, the angel gabriel.

the evening light, the west, the east.

the train, the streetcar from the west.

the many towers of the town.

we don't know where the light comes from.

the sun appears, the ancient stars.

we sleep, we wake,

we learn, we teach,

give birth and work.

we don't know when the light goes out.

we know the morning comes again.

we don't know where the light comes from.

August 2011

布拉格：礼拜天的犹太区

风琴和唱诗班开唱

房子里的人死了

银行里的人死了

邮局里的人死了

城里的房子旧了

大街和小巷旧了

风琴和唱诗班开唱

镇上来的孩子死了

镇上来的老人死了

镇上来的女人死了

镇上来的男人死了

风琴和唱诗班开唱

教堂里的天使死了

光明中的使者死了

黑暗中的雕像死了

大街和小巷旧了

城里的房子旧了

风琴和唱诗班开唱

2011.10

PRAGUE: JEWISH QUARTER ON A SUNDAY

the organ and the choir begin
the people in the house are dead
the people at the bank are dead
the people at the post are dead
the houses in the town are old
the alleys and the streets are old

the organ and the choir begin
the children from the town are dead
the old ones from the town are dead
the women from the town are dead
the menfolk from the town are dead

the organ and the choir begin
the angels in the church are dead
the figures in the light are dead
the figures in the dark are dead
the alleys and the streets are old
the houses in the town are old

the organ and the choir begin

October 2011

落叶纷纷

仅仅在数天之内
树叶是红的
仅仅在数天之内
树叶全都泛黄
仅仅在数天之内
雪花还在翻筋斗
仅仅在数天之内
今天已经很暖和

也就几分钟
月亮便升起
也就几分钟
你还看得很清晰
也就几分钟
我们在光下畅饮
也就几分钟
我们将离去

2011.11

FALL

in just a few days
leaves are all red
in just a few days
leaves are all yellow
in just a few days
snow's doing cartwheels
in just a few days
today is still mild

for just a few minutes
moon's on the rise
for just a few minutes
you still see quite well
for just a few minutes
let's drink in the light
for just a few minutes
we are leaving soon

November 2011

月亮重临

歌声

歌声、树影、月亮、夜晚

街道、车辆，月光明亮

空气怡人，一颗孤星在那里闪耀

我希望我们睡个通宵

2011.12

MOON AGAIN

song

the song the tree the moon the night

the streets the cars the moon is bright

the air is right one star is there

i hope we sleep all through the night

December 2011

暮色四合

紧裹并倾听
倾听雨夜
现在请你抱紧我
风儿摇着盛开的树
长夜将逝雨不休
没关系，我们近在眼前
没关系，我们远在天边
我们远在天边
远在天边
天差地别
倾听雨夜
没关系，我们近在眼前
靠近疯狂靠近愤怒
靠近破坏靠近黄金
把自己裹在雨中
把思想裹在风中
我与你近在眼前
我与你远在天边
我与你天差地别

2012.3

LATE NITE WRAP

wrap and listen
listen to the rainy night
wrap yourself around me now
wind will sway the blooming tree
night will pass and rain may stay
it's alright we're very close
it's alright we're very far
we were rather far away
far around and far ahead
far behind and far between
listen to the rainy night
it's alright we're very close
close to madness close to rage
close to breaking close to gold
wrap yourself around the rain
wrap your mind around the wind
i am very close to you
i am very far behind
i was rather far away

March, 2012

海

海是光明。
海是声音。
海是洁白。
海是回旋。
海是空气。
海是大地。
海是头发。
海是发现。
海是公正。
海是死亡。
海是嶙峋。
海是呼吸。
海是深邃。
海是肌肤。
海是黄金。
海是蔚蓝。
海被出卖。
树木泪湿。
海是古老。

海是时间。
海是泡沫。
海是黑暗。
海是韵律。
海是飓风。
海是强壮。
海是善良。
海是错误。
海是天空。
海是紧张。
海是黑麦。
海是正义。
海是空间。
海是声音。
海是光明。

2012.7

SEA

the sea is light.
the sea is sound.
the sea is white.
the sea is round.
the sea is air.
the sea is ground.
the sea is hair.
the sea is found.
the sea is fair.
the sea is death.
the sea is thin.
the sea is breath.
the sea is deep.
the sea is skin.
the sea is gold.
the sea is blue.
the sea is sold.
the trees are wet.
the sea is old.

the sea is time.

the sea is foam.

the sea is dark.

the sea is rhyme.

the sea is wind.

the sea is strong.

the sea is kind.

the sea is wrong.

the sea is sky.

the sea is tight.

the sea is rye.

the sea is right.

the sea is space.

the sea is sound.

the sea is light.

July 2012

摩洛哥喷泉

——维也纳“摩洛哥乐园”

太阳正汗涔涔地反射着马赛克。

喷泉因破碎而被关闭。

人们大都很忙。

现在是上午九点钟。

购物，吸烟。

高跟鞋。也许有点用。

缩在外套和围巾中。

与前几日相比，天气很冷。

太阳转瞬即逝。

这温暖的早晨的太阳。

2012.8

MOROCCAN FOUNTAIN

—marokkanergasse, vienna

the sun is streaming against the mosaic.

the fountain's broken, turned off.

the people are busy, most of them.

it's 9 am.

shopping, smoking.

high heels. maybe productive.

in jackets and scarves.

it's chilly compared with a few days ago.

for a moment, the sun.

the warm morning sun.

August 2012

在火车上看月亮

起初月亮很大
起初月亮几乎不在那儿
我们看到它从火车上升起
上面一弯，下面一弯
一定是月亮出来了
他们说很圆很满
看起来不满四分之一
月亮出来了，火车继续前进
火车上人满为患，车厢很短
火车上全是疲惫不堪的人
空气糟糕，厕所被堵
接着月亮重临
火车穿过多瑙河大桥
徒步旅行的日子真美
田野、树林、小径、美酒
天气晴好，月亮隐去
我希望远在天涯的友人
在月下都感觉美好

2012.9

MOON FROM TRAIN

the moon was very big at first
the moon at first was hardly there
we saw it rising from the train
one strip above, one strip below
must be the moon, it will come out
they say it's very full and round
it doesn't look a quarter full
the moon comes out, the train moves on
the train is full and rather short
the tired people on the train
the air is bad, the bathroom's blocked
and then the moon comes out again
the train has crossed the danube bridge
the hiking day was beautiful
the fields, the woods, the paths, the wine
the day was fine, the moon is gone
i hope our friends across the world
are feeling well around the moon.

September 2012

在肖普朗[1]古老的犹太教堂里

欧罗巴的背面是怎样的景象。一个自由的、毫无安全感的所在。在碎片和屠宰场里，空旷，死寂。但记忆能够呼吸并且歌唱。

2014.4

[1] 肖普朗：匈牙利的一座小城。——译注

OLD SYNAGOGUE IN SOPRON

europe is what lies behind. a space for freedom, insecurity. in shards and shambles, empty, dead. yet memory may breathe and sing.

April 2014

捷克克鲁姆洛夫教堂

一切皆为人类所创造
只有光来自上帝
以及灵感
还有大白天带手电筒的孩子
他来自我

2014.4

CATHEDRAL IN ČESKÝ KRUMLOV[1]

everything is made by people
only light comes from god
and inspiration
and a boy with a flashlight by day
comes from me

April 2014

---

[1] 本诗先有德语版，后有英语版。德语原诗为：

KATHEDRALE IN KRUMAU

alles ist von menschen gemacht
nur das licht ist von gott
und die inspiration
und ein bub mit der lampe am hellichten tag
der ist von mir

April 2014

基训河[1]

基训之水天上来
奔流到强生镇我们小窗下不复回。
亚当与夏娃同居了多长时间?
也许四周，抑或没那么久。
继而他们被汽车载到下一个机场。
是那条蛇。是那棵树。
是那只苹果。是出售苹果酒的
加油站。还有中餐馆。
上帝其实是个快乐的老爷子
告诉各位他们如何创建了这座伊甸园。
上帝宽容大度，上帝虚怀若谷。
也许是一百年前工匠们
建造了他们的教堂，留下他们——
逆时针行走、数字倒置的钟

---

[1] 《圣经》伊甸园第二道河基训河："第二道河名叫基训，就是环绕古实全地的。"(《创世记》2:13)"基训"的原文意思是"川流溢满"，这里还蕴含着"骄傲，值得较量"之意。神早就预知从基训河流域发祥的文明将会铮铮佼佼。发源于美国东北部格林山脉流经佛蒙特创作中心的小河也叫基训河。——译注

杂货店里就有一个这样的钟——

也许工匠们就像嬉皮士。

无论如何如果你在天堂

大多时光过着俗人的日子。

你告诉你的妻子你在天堂。

你告诉你的丈夫，你告诉你的孩子。

他们会说好，希望你早日回家。

然后你就滚了。也许你会再来。

只有一点我敢肯定：此河将滔滔不绝，长流不息。

2014.10

GIHON

gihon is one of the waters of paradise
under our windows in johnson town.
how long did adam and eve have their residence?
maybe four weeks. not even that.
then they were driven to the next airport.
it was the snake. it was the tree.
it was the apple. it was the gas station
stocked with the cider. the chinese restaurant.
actually god is a jolly old fellow
tells everyone how they founded the place.
god has the breadth. god has the width of it.
maybe the masons one hundred years ago
building their temple, leaving their clocks—
there is that clock down in the grocery store
clock that goes leftwards, numbers all turned—
maybe the masons were like the hippies.
anyway if you are in paradise
most of the time it is just life.
you tell your wife you are in paradise.

you tell your husband, you tell the kids.

they will say nice, hope you are coming back.

then you are gone. maybe you come again.

i'm sure the river stays for a while.

October 2014

月亮

一片柠檬

一片蜜橘

一块姜黄色的蛋糕

最终我们赢得了雪

2014.12

MOON

a slice of lemon

a slice of tangerine

a ginger cake

finally we have snow

December 2014

风

大风天

观察风

仰望普照万物的太阳

塑料袋

云彩

远处某物看起来像一面旗帜

红色和白色[1]

一切都不过是一阵风

2015.1

---

1 奥地利国旗由红色和白色构成。——译注

WIND

windy day

watching the wind

watching the sun moving on things

plastic wraps

clouds

something in the distance looks like a flag

red and white

let it be just the wind

January 2015

好

望着乘地铁的人们。
他们是好人吗?
他们在床上活儿好吗?
也许该把他们绑起来?
这些问题太复杂了。

2015.9

GOOD

look at the people riding the subway.

are they good people?

are they good in bed?

maybe tie them up?

it would be all too complicated.

September 2015

鲜花

我还在为巴黎祈祷
十天后
我为维也纳祈祷
在法国领事馆旁
是苏军纪念碑
我坐 D 路电车经过它
每年纪念碑下都有花圈
这是今年以来的第二次
鲜花包围了领事馆
每一次天都愈冷
伊拉克再次发现大规模坟墓
这一次是老年妇女
照“脸书”上所说
她们不易被拐卖
统计数字可能是精确的
苏军纪念碑为了欧洲和平
许多希腊石柱
刻满斯大林诗文
还有一个大喷泉

水来自阿尔卑斯山
输水渠的建筑师
让维也纳生机勃勃
让鲜花一年年盛开
他是犹太人

2015.11

FLOWERS

i am still praying for paris
ten days later
i pray for vienna
next to the french consulate
is the soviet monument
i pass it in streetcar d
there are wreaths at the monument every year
there are flowers all around the consulate
second time this year
every time it gets cold
mass graves detected again in iraq
this time elderly women
according to facebook
who could not be sold easily
probably accurate
the soviet monument to peace in europe
lots of greek columns
inscribed by stalin
and a big fountain

with water straight from the alps

the architect of the aqueduct

that keeps vienna alive

let it bloom again and again

was a jew

November 2015

塔尔巴克和德雷夫黑文

我有生以来从未见过这么多鹿
从未见过这么多，这么多鹿
爬上那座古老城堡四周的小山
赫米塔日狩猎小屋
像一座小美景宫
我意思是维也纳的美景宫
但这是森林，
荒凉至极
在一个大城市附近。
这是一个很神奇的地方。
牛羊成群。
有些牧群有大鹿角
有些鹿是黑色的。
有些是纯白。
大部分鹿是棕色的，正如我所知道的那样。
我以前从未见过白鹿。
也没有见过一群鹿全都长着这样的鹿角。
也许是小麋鹿。
不知道该怎么称呼它们。

有人经过，

人们骑自行车，

穿过它们。

我和它们有点不同。

如果它们冲过来攻击，

我们该怎么办?

我女儿玛雅不害怕，

她径直向它们走去。

离它们只有几米远了，

然后它们撤退。

有些小家伙，

不害羞。

两只非常小的鹿，

我们在它们和它们的母亲之间。

我想知道如果一个受伤了，

如果一个生病了，会发生什么?

它们关心彼此吗?

每年都有猎鹿者，

我们听说。

有一个谷仓，

也许储藏着冬天的粮食。

克里斯蒂安在路边给我们看薄荷。

这是一次漫长的夜晚散步，
虽然走得不远。
你看到大海，你听到火车，
你甚至听到警报声
在森林外路上的某个地方。
这是一段漫长而神奇的散步。
如果你住在这里，离鹿那么近，
距大海那么近。
你会有一个美好的幸运的生活。
还有一件事：维基百科说
1854 年 6 月 5 日
三万人
庆贺宪法诞生
在赫米塔日狩猎小屋前
我不知道鹿怎么看那件事。

2016.8

TAARBAEK AND DYREHAVEN

never seen so many deer in my life

never seen so many, so many deer

up on the hill round the old castle

hermitage hunting lodge

little bit like a small belvedere

i mean the belvedere in vienna

but this is the forest,

as wild as it gets

next to a big city.

this is a very magical place.

herds upon herds.

some of the herds all have great antlers

some deer are black.

some are all white.

most deer are brown, as i have known them.

but i have never seen white deer before

nor seen a herd all with such antlers.

maybe small elks.

don’t know how they’re called.

people walk by,

people ride through them,

riding on bicycles.

i am a little vary of them.

if they came charging,

what would we do?

my daughter maia is not afraid,

she walks right up to them.

some are a few meters away,

then they withdraw.

there are small kids,

not very shy.

two very small deer,

we are between them and their mother.

i wonder what happens if one is injured,

if one is sick.

do they care for each other?

once a year there are hunters,

we hear.

there is a barn,

maybe food for the winter.

kristian shows us mint by the road.

this is a long walk in the evening,
though it's not very far.
you see the sea, you hear the train,
you even hear sirens
somewhere on roads outside the forest.
it was a long, magical walk.
if you live here, so close to the deer,
so close to the sea
you have a wonderful, privileged life.
one more thing: wikipedia says
the constitution was celebrated
june 5, 1854
30,000 people
in front of hermitage hunting lodge
i wonder what the deer thought of that.

August 2016

奥地利

奥地利
让奥地利人
露出最坏的一面
根据我身为奥地利人
的经验
但你永远不会知道

2016.11

AUSTRIA

austria

brings out the worst

in austrians

from my experience

as an austrian

but you never know

November 2016

诗

诗

是重

要的

真理

是无

能的

或者它是

或者你是

2017.2

POETRY

poetry

is impo

rtant

truth

is impo

tent

or is it

or are you

February 2017

报道

每一份报道
详尽尖锐的报道
使强权者不安的那种报道
都与其他任何艺术
任何诗
任何教堂、庙宇
同样重要
那让你停顿
思考
感觉
的每一份报道

2017.2

REPORT

every report

every detailed incisive report

kind that makes powerful people squirm

is just as important

as any art

any poem

any church, temple

that makes you pause

think

feel

every report

February 2017

十二岁

早晨的太阳
一根红条子
在我们房间的墙上
孩子们醒来
女儿洗头
儿子在厕所
跑回到床上
像一头大象
明天他就十二岁了
我感觉到你脖子上脉搏的跳动
起床去做早餐

2017.3

12

in the morning the sun
a red sliver
on the wall in our room
the kids are awake
daughter washing her hair
son on the toilet
runs back to bed
like an elephant
tomorrow he's 12
i feel the pulse in your neck
and get up to make breakfast

March 2017

写诗

你必须敞开心扉
面对不同的事物
你必须敞开心扉
面对美好的事物
有时
某事
猛冲，
打击。
你必须打开自己
停下你的步履
除此你什么都不必做。

2017.4

TO WRITE A POEM

you have to be open
to something different
you have to be open
to something good
sometimes
something
that hurtles,
that hurts.
you have to be open
to hold your step.
you don't have to be anything.

April 2017

在奥地利

我们有个十四岁的孩子
被残忍地杀害
从背后射杀
被一个
身为警察
仍在服役的
凶手

2017.4

IN AUSTRIA

we have a 14-year-old

who was brutally killed

shot in the back

by a murderer

who still serves

as policeman

April 2017

俄斯特拉发[1]

大城
砂砾
维特科维采
炼铁厂
科学博物馆
站在 CT 扫描机前
缓缓移动你的手臂
它显示了你的内部
从脚向上
骨骼、肌肉、脂肪
等等
男性或者女性
你意识到这其实
不是你的身体
它是个囚犯
他们砍了他 2000 刀

1 捷克城市。

砍了她 2500 刀

它在美国

伟大的博物馆

非常友善的人民

十分适合度假

2017.5

OSTRAVA

great city

gritty

vitkovice

iron works

science museum

stand in front of the ct scan

move your arm slowly

it shows you the inside

from the feet up

bones, muscles, fat

and so on

male or female

you realize it's not

actually your body

it was a prisoner

they cut him 2,000 times

her 2,500 times

it was in america

great museum

very friendly people

very good for a holiday

May 2017

夜深人静

夜深人静

月儿开始歌唱

当她酒酣之际

便躲在云儿后面

2017.6

SOME TIME LATE AT NIGHT

some time late at night

the moon starts to sing

when she's full of drink

and hides behind clouds

June 2017

玛丽亚·圣雷斯迪图塔·卡夫卡

她一定是最重要的塑像
在这座大教堂里
但她在后面
在侧室
你可以进去祈祷

只要待在里面
你便不再是目瞪口呆的旅游者
只有上帝看见你在凝视

起先你看到耶稣
你什么都不想说
虽然没人阻止你
拍照

房间感觉很古老
比大教堂
更现代

她多大?

在纳粹杀害她的时候

在维也纳此处的

大法院

她是一个修女，一个护士

来自布尔诺胡索维采

在维也纳长大

在莫德林服务

现存的教堂有现代的事物

它显然不在这里

只是与此相得益彰

她一定是迄今为止最重要的人物

在科希策大教堂有一个人

在靠近入口处的地方

你一眼就看到她了

在科希策有成千上万犹太人

在维也纳超过五万

何谓上帝
何谓祈祷
何谓人
何谓圣徒

与上帝同行

2017.7

MARIA RESTITUTA KAFKA

she must be the most important statue
in this great cathedral
but she's in the back
in a side room
you can go in for prayer

as long as you're in there
you're no gaping tourist
only god sees you gaping

at first you see jesus
you don't want to say much at all
although no one stops you
from taking a photo

the room feels more ancient
and more contemporary
than the cathedral at large

how old was she

when the nazis killed her

at the big courthouse

here in vienna?

she was a sister, a nurse

came from husovice, brno

grew up in vienna

and served in mödling

living churches have modern things

it's not in your face here

but it fits well

she must be the most important person by far

there is one in kosice

next to an entrance

you notice her right away

thousands of jews in kosice

over fifty-thousand here in vienna

what is god

what is prayer

what is a person

what is a saint

go with god

July 2017

夏夜

夏天的夜晚
月亮是一个白色的足球
在公园上空晃来晃去
它在黄昏中
溶解
又在黑暗中出来
与蝉相伴
我们好运多多
杏子饺子
葡萄酒
我们身体健康
祝愿人人
都有一个好月亮

2017.7

SUMMER EVENING

summer evening

moon is a white soccer ball

dangling over the park

it dissolves

in the twilight

comes out in the dark

with cicadas

we are very very lucky

apricot dumplings

wine

we are healthy

wish everyone

had a good moon

July 2017

巴塞罗那蒙特惠奇山

蒙特惠奇山意味着
漫山遍野的犹太墓地。
在 1380 年代
犹太人被驱赶
出城市，
墓碑被占用
作了城墙。
一千年前
矗立起一座灯塔。
后来城堡建在山顶
经常被用来炮打全城。
有充分的理由，
有充分的历史原因
可以独立。
到处都讲
加泰罗尼亚语，
加泰罗尼亚语第一，西班牙语第二。
城堡给你
上了一堂历史课

以希伯来语开头
还有一首加泰罗尼亚语诗。
城市的大部分建筑
由此处的
山石建造。
今天有了和平，
足以用来反思。
你的需要有多少，
可以合作的是多少，
可以团结的是多少，
经济学占多少，
公共交通占多少……
从山顶
你能看见什么？

2017.7

MONTJUIC, BARCELONA

montjuic means
mountain of the jewish cemetery.
in the 1380s
the jews were driven
out of the city,
gravestones were used
for castle walls.
1,000 years ago
there was a light house.
later the castles built on the top
were often used to shoot on the city.
there's an ample reason,
there are ample historical reasons
for independence.
catalan language
is everywhere,
catalan first, spanish second.
the castle gives you
a history lesson

beginning in hebrew
and a poem in catalan.
much of the city
was built from quarries
here on the mountain.
today there is peace,
enough for reflection.
how much do you need,
how much cooperation,
how much solidarity,
how much economics,
how much is public transport...
what can you see
from the top of the mountain?

July 2017

之一

生命中最美好的事物之一就是感觉到你
生命中最美好的事物之一在早晨
生命中最美好的事物之一就是感觉到你
生命中最美好的事物之一在晚上
生命中最美好的事物之一就是看见你
生命中最美好的事物之一在光里
生命中最美好的事物之一就是认识你
我在这个地球上所知道的最美好的事物之一
生命中最美好的事物之一就是拥抱你
拥抱你意味着
没有别的东西
什么也没有
只有风
鸟群
火车
孩子们的
啼哭
街的对面
或者隔壁

有太阳

温暖的一天

去看看孩子们在干吗

2017.7

ONE OF

one of the best things in life is to feel you
on of the best things of life in the morning
one of the best things in life is to feel you
one of the best things of life in the night
one of the best things in life is to see you
one of the best things of life in the light
one of the best things in life is to know you
one of the best things i know on this earth
one of the best things in life is to hold you
holding you means
no other thing
there is nothing
there is the wind
birds
a train
cries
of the children
across the street
or next door

there is the sun

warmth of the day

got to see what the children are up to

July 2017

明信片

我们在巴基奥。
生活是完美的。
生活是危险的，像在任何地方。
生活是完美的。
波涛汹涌。
气候特殊。
并不太热。
我们从巴塞罗那
来到毕尔巴鄂。
在这个地区，历史
也意味着
反抗和独立。
巴基奥有一位新的左派市长。
巴基奥是一个中等规模的城市。
避暑别墅。
夏日公寓。
一年到头都很满。
冬天里的波涛更加汹涌。
海洋索回

古老的海岸线。

生活是完美的。

圣胡安教堂

在那块不远处的岩石上

如果你急赶

徒步需要两小时

在《权力的游戏》中。

那里只剩下一座宫殿。

待会儿见！

2017.8

POSTCARD

we are in bakio.

life is perfect.

life is precarious, as everywhere.

life is perfect.

waves.

special climate.

not too hot.

we came to bilbao

from barcelona.

in this region, too

history means

resistance and independence.

bakio has a new leftist mayor.

bakio is a mid-sized town.

summer houses.

summer apartments.

some things all year.

bigger waves in winter.

the sea claims back

the old beachline.

life is perfect.

the church of san juan

up on that rock not very far

two hours on foot

less if you hurry

is in game of thrones.

only there it's a palace.

see you soon!

August 2017

为安妮·洛尔和诺埃尔而作

人是玫瑰，人是树叶。
婚姻是
种花，
耕田，
修理拖拉机。
或者使用另外一种东西。
经验会帮到你们，
虽然你们总是希望
第一次就能成功。
人是花儿，人是星星。
婚姻是
依靠
彼此，
还有各自的朋友和家人。
安妮·洛尔和诺埃尔，
我们祝你们像月亮
和太阳一般永远
像它们一样美丽。
我们爱你。保重！

2017.8

FOR ANNE-LAURE AND NOEL

people are roses, people are leaves.
marriage is
planting a flower,
tilling a field,
repairing a tractor.
or using another one.
experience helps,
although you always hope
it works the first time.
people are flowers, people are stars.
marriage is
falling
back on each other,
each other' s friends and family.
anne-laure and noel,
we wish you the moon
and the sun forever
as beautiful as they are here.
we love you. take care!

August 2017

蒙娜丽莎

微笑的人儿
被悉心保护
她永远挂在
一座崭新的
由日本电视台赞助的监狱中
每日到访
数以百万人
他们全都是凡人
无人在意他们是否微笑
除了其中一些人的
很短的片刻

2017.8

MONA LISA

the smiling one
is well protected
she hangs forever
in a brand-new prison
supported by nippon television
visited daily
by millions of people
all of them mortal
no-one cares if they smile
except some of them
for a very short while

August 2017

奥地利国庆节

2017 年
奥地利国庆节
是个美丽的日子
我们排着队站在英雄广场
沿着城堡
只为进入总统的官邸
队伍中跟在我们身后的
是一个叙利亚男孩
他的德语很好
给我看他手机里
他用德语写的东西
听起来仿佛来自十九世纪
但却清楚而又正确
骨瘦如柴的小家伙
不知道他的家人
是否仍在叙利亚
至少他可以留在这里
在阿拉伯语中
有十二个或更多的词可以表达爱

他自译成
德语或英语
他感觉相当笨手笨脚
走进皇宫内部
总统办公室
安保不是很严格
我们的导游来自办公室
在她典型的
奥地利人的发音中
声音听起来骄傲又超然
还有点讽刺意味
在同一时间
我们没有逮到总统
但我们看到了女皇
她相貌平平
却是最强大的女人
玛丽亚 · 特蕾西娅
如今这里只是
总统接待政府官员的房间
是的，它比从电视里看小得多
建筑内部有暖气
在帝国时期

所有中间的过道
空气流通
一路通往地下室
在当时非常先进
只有一个房间
拥有壁炉
这个房间有十五摄氏度
冬天里的十五摄氏度
这是整座建筑中最温暖的宫殿
欧洲最大的城堡
国庆节，奥地利军队
气氛相当放松
每个人都能
喝茶，听好音乐
在总统的庭院中
陆军乐队，演奏很好的爵士乐，
当然还有施特劳斯圆舞曲
孩子们爬上
国家纪念碑
奥地利国庆节
没什么值得夸耀的
至少总统不是

德国民族主义者

去年不容易

所有这些选举

今年还要更糟糕

明年这些混蛋

将进入政府

这是一个美好的国庆节

这是一个美丽的国家

2017.10

AUSTRIAN NATIONAL DAY

austrian national day

2017

it's a beautiful day

we stand in line on heroes' square

along the castle

to get into the president's quarters

next to us in line

is a guy from syria

his german is very good

he hands me his phone

what he writes in german

sounds like 19th century

but it's clear and correct

a small scrawny guy

don't know if his family

is still in syria

at least he can stay

there are 12 words or more

for love in arabic

translating himself

into german or english

he feels rather clumsy

going inside the imperial palace

the president's office

security is not very strict

our guide from the office

in her typical

austrian diction

sounds proud and detached

and somewhat ironic

at the same time

we don't catch the president

but we see the empress

she looks ordinary

the most powerful woman

maria theresia

now this is the room

where the president receives the government

yes, it's much smaller than on tv

there was heating inside the building

in imperial times

the whole middle tract
air going up and down
all the way to the basement
very advanced for the time
only one room
has a fireplace
they had 15 degrees in this room
15 celsius in winter
this was the warmest place in the building
the largest castle in europe
national day, austrian army
the atmosphere is rather relaxed
tea and good music
for everyone
in the president's courtyard
regional army band, very good jazz
and of course strauss
children climbing
national monuments
austrian national day
nothing to brag about
at least the president

is not a german nationalist

last year wasn't easy

all those elections

this year is much worse

next year those fuckers

will be in government

it was a nice national day

it's a beautiful country

October 2017

你

你默许这头猿

这头臭气熏天污秽满身

比任何动物都更糟糕的猿

你助这头笑嘻嘻的

怪物

这个新纳粹摇身一变

成愤怒失败者的主宰

自由愤怒的失败者

大吵大闹

一切为了强壮

保护

反对

良心

团结

觉悟

他们的所作所为

他们如何让你压迫

弱者

这意味着你

你自己的家人

有时候随波逐流

总是

比你想象的要快

别思考

快投票

为这头笑嘻嘻

强壮的猿

2017.10

YOU

you allowed this ape
this strong-reeking filth
worse than any animal
you helped this grinning
creep
this neo-nazi turned
lord of angry losers
free angry losers
free-for-all
all for strong
protection
against
conscience
solidarity
consciousness
of what they do
how they make you screw
the weak
which means you
your own family

sometimes down the road

always

sooner than you think

don’t think

vote

for the grinning

strong

October 2017

改变

我想如果你常有机会更换国家
那就太好了
学匈牙利语
可以教英文德文中文
中国当代诗歌中任何有用的东西
不是因为你真的必须如此
而是以一种旋转变幻的方式
那么重返年轻
也许会很好
但这只会在梦中发生
我过着美好的生活
改变你的性别
只一小会儿
也会很有趣
无论如何
有时不同的国家
几乎对每个人来说
不单是为了旅行
都是伟大的

对世界和平来说
那么有多少沧海
被成吉思汗变成桑田
我老婆问

2017.11

CHANGE

i think it would be good if you could
change your country more often
learn hungarian
maybe teach english german chinese
current chinese poetry anything useful
not because you really have to
but in a kind of rotating fashion
then it would also be very good
to be young again
but that happens in dreams
and i've had a good life
to change your gender
just for a while
would be interesting too
anyway
a different country
for almost anyone once in a while
not just travelling
would be great

for world peace

so how many things

did genghis khan change

asks my wife

November 2017

轻音乐

我的阳台上有一盏美丽的灯，
是某种橘色的像腐烂的叶子，
万圣节的面具慢慢地坍塌，
不再是脸的样子除非你事先知道
这是一个多雾的日子，但生活是美丽的，
室外的人们幸福而稀少。
有时你无法确定他们是男还是女，
在远处看，他们只是一个图形。
有时有来自远方的汽车的灯光，
通常情况下，什么都没有。
我们住在新火车站后面，
市中心以南，砌砖工人聚居区。
火车南站，南边或东南边，
货车修理厂，也许还有兔子，
兔子待在公园外面
他们仍在建造那里。
所有这些空间都属于铁路，
一个铁路人仍然领导着这个国家，
社会党，诞生于这个地区。

一个铁路经理，
美好的三十年
他们希望管理者领导社会主义者，
管理者住着工会房子
在第一区。
人们仍会为他们投票，
有一个可怕的大选，
受到社会主义者的帮助
通过免费报纸的
广告。
等铁路工人认识到这些
至少晚了三十年。
我阳台上有一盏美丽的灯，
橙色野花和腐烂物，
美丽的东西明年还会长出来。

2017.11

LIGHT MUSIC

there is a beautiful light on my balcony,
orange somehow like rotten leaves,
halloween faces slowly crumbling,
no longer faces except when you know
it is a foggy day but life is beautiful,
people outside are blessedly few.
sometimes you're not sure if they're male or female,
farther away, they're just a figure.
sometimes there are lights from faraway cars,
most often there's nothing.
we live behind the new railway station,
south of the center, bricklayer's district.
south railway station, south or southeast,
freight cars repairs, probably rabbits,
rabbits remain beyond the park
where they're still building.
all this space belonged to the railways,
a railway man still heads the country,
socialist party, born in this district.

a railway manager,

good thirty years now

they wanted managers leading the socialists,

managers living in union housing

in the first district.

still people vote for them,

there is a big gruesome alternative,

helped by the socialists

through advertising

in the free newspapers.

railway man realized that

thirty years late at least.

there is a beautiful light on my balcony,

orange wildflowers and rotten stuff,

beautiful things come out next year.

November 2017

静夜谣

和我们一起唱歌
和我们一起歌唱
和我们坐在一起
和我们一起用餐
让我们再次相聚
让我们再次欢聚
坐在天庭唱歌
坐在天庭歌唱

2017.12

SILENT NIGHT

sing with us

sing with us

sit with us

eat with us

let us be together again

let us be together again

sit in heaven and sing

sit in heaven and sing

December 2017

个人简历

维马丁
不是犹太人
他的孩子们
还没有完全长大
除此之外
他是他能记得的
有争议的
最伟大的诗人
出生于
1966 年
在中国
创作
但他生在维也纳
比他的父母
拥有更舒适的童年，
学习
然后去了台湾
研究
在上海捣蛋，

初遇妻子，
教难民，
在西安和武汉再遇妻子，
去了罗马尼亚，
在那里遇到中国朋友，
娶妻，
去了重庆，
然后在北京一直待到 2008 年。
两个孩子生在那儿。
翻译宣传资料，
写作，翻译
越来越多的
诗歌
也翻译其他材料
直到现在
在维也纳，
2018 年
还有几天。
干杯！

2017.12

PS：翻译作品被《纽约时报》、《纽约书评》、《南华早报》、《澳大利亚流浪者新闻》、《台北时报》、《顿悟》、佛蒙特创作中心、图森桂冠诗人丽贝卡·塞弗勒采用。翻译成德语的作品发表于新泽西《新苏黎世报》《法兰克福汇报》和诸多论文和杂志。与在奥地利的中国诗人和 Esther Dischereit、Agnes Schick 等人一起组织过活动。“NPC李白诗歌奖·翻译奖”得主。在中国和奥地利出版的书籍贡献给诗，其他文本与翻译给了各地的德语、英语、中文书籍与杂志。如果需要会给出名目。再干一杯，愿力量与反抗同在。是的，真的。谢谢你们！

CV

martin winter

is not jewish

and his children

are not fully grown

otherwise

he is arguably

the greatest poet

he can remember,

born

in 1966

cr

in china

but he was born in vienna

and had a much more comfortable childhood

than his parents,

studied

then went to taiwan

studied

did mischief in shanghai,

met wife,

taught refugees,

met wife again in xi’an and wuhan,

went to romania,

met chinese friends there,

married wife,

they went to chongqing,

then stayed in beijing till 2008.

two children born there.

translated propaganda,

wrote, translated

more and more

poetry

among other stuff

until now

in vienna,

2018

in a few days.

cheers!

December 2017

P.S. Translations were used by *NY Times*, *NY Review of Books*, *South China Morning Post*, *Australia Vagabond Press*, *Taipei Times*, *Epiphany*, Vermont Studio Center, Tucson poetry laureate Rebecca Seiferle. Translations into German appeared in *Neue Zürcher Zeitung (NZZ)*, *Frankfurter Allgemeine Zeitung (FAZ)* and many papers and magazines. Organized events with Chinese poets in Austria, together with Esther Dischereit, Agnes Schick, and others. Recipient of Li Bai Poetry Prize for Translation. Published books in China and Austria, contributed poems, other texts and translations to books and magazines in German, English and Chinese in many places. Will give details if needed. Cheers again, may the force be with the resistance. Yes, seriously. Thank you!

尤尔斯明讷：我们，泡沫

我们是泡沫，滚动的泡沫
旋转的气泡，叫骂的声音
跳舞的昆虫，闪烁的草坪
摇曳的花朵，低语的树叶。
我们是风，起泡的风
赶走乌云，沸扬的光
吹走石头，燃烧星星
咬牙切齿的孩子们，闪闪烁烁的夜晚
黏土是我们，咆哮的黏土

2018.2

JUELSMINDE: WE, FOAM

foam are we, rolling foam
whirling bubbles, hurling sound
dancing insects, blinking grass
rocking blossoms, whispering leaves.
wind are we, foaming wind
driving clouds, simmering light
blowing rocks, burning stars
gnashing children, flickering night
clay are we, snarling clay

February 2018

金凤花

金凤花
是一个卡通人。
她不是很娇俏，
但她是个女孩，毫无疑问。
我们不知道她有名字，
所以我们称她为魔鬼的仆人。
他对她有某种控制力，
不确定到底是什么。
她总是想做苹果汁。
那是她的职业，
她在一家苹果汁工厂干活。
她试图逃跑，
但她不得不遵从魔鬼的使唤。
所以她绑架了橡皮鸭子。
没错，这一切都发生在浴缸里。
她比他大，但这从来都不重要。
我们在北京有一个浴缸，一件奢侈品。
不是很大。
我们搬到维也纳时，浴缸变大了，玛雅长大了。
现在她弟弟在浴缸里玩。

2018.2

BUTTERCUP

buttercup

is an action figure.

she's not very dainty,

but she's a girl, no doubt about it.

we didn't know she had a name,

so we called her the devil's servant.

he had some kind of hold over her,

not sure what exactly.

she always wanted to make apple juice.

that was her calling,

she worked in an apple juice factory.

she tried to escape and go back,

but she had to do the devil's bidding.

so she kidnapped rubber ducks.

that's right, all this takes place in the bathtub.

she is bigger than him, but that was never important.

we had a bathtub in beijing, a luxury.

not very big.

when we moved to vienna, bathtubs got bigger, and maia grew up.

now her brother plays in the bathtub.

February 2018

马里博尔犹太教堂

马里博尔的犹太教堂
空空荡荡。
感觉像一座教堂，
建于六百多年前，
一部分城墙
紧靠河边。
它已经空了五百年。
斯特里亚省的犹太人
被马克西米利安驱逐出境。
也许他不能偿还其债。
他们办了一个展览
关于来自普里莫尔的，
本地犹太人。
有些在来自奥斯威辛的
照片上。
照片是德国人拍的。
一个十分可爱的金发少女。
没有孩子幸存下来。
有一张幸存者的照片，
被人带回穆斯卡·苏波卡

或者类似的地方。
不知道现在那里还有什么。
有一种尊严
在幸存者中。
犹太教堂
古老而空旷。
中世纪窗户
像蜡烛
或剪影一样
又长又细，
仿佛房顶的火焰。
还有一个中央窗口，
高耸的圆圈
由小圆圈构成。
入场费一欧元，
团体免费。
包括说明书
和讲解在内。
空空荡荡的犹太教堂，
许多城市的
地标建筑。

2018.3

MARIBOR SYNAGOGUE

the synagogue of maribor

is an empty church.

feels like a church,

built over 600 years ago,

part of the city wall

next to the river.

it has been empty for 500 years.

jews were expelled by maximilian

from the whole province,

the province of styria.

maybe he couldn't pay his debts.

they have an exhibition

about jews from primorje,

a local region.

some are on photos

from auschwitz.

photos taken by germans.

a very cute fair-haired girl.

no children survived.

there is a photo of survivors,

back in murska subotka

or something like that.

don't know if there are any there now.

there is a dignity

in the survivors.

the synagogue

is old and empty.

medieval windows

like candles

or silhouettes.

long and thin,

on top like a flame.

and a central window,

a circle high up

made from small circles.

entrance is one euro,

or free for groups.

explanations

and stories included.

the empty synagogue,

a major landmark

in many cities.

March 2018

把你的声音放低

把你的声音放低
我父亲说
每当
我和我侄子说话
在复活节或圣诞节
没有人再那么说过
除了我妻子偶尔为之
至少他没有说
别把胳膊肘放在桌子上
白打我来到知天命之年
我们是这样对待自己的后代的吗
当然我们是不同的
就让他们写下我们的事
随着时间的推移

2018.4

KEEP YOUR VOICE DOWN

keep your voice down
says my father
every time
when i finally get to talk to my nephews
at easter or christmas
nobody ever says that
except my wife once in a while
at least he doesn't say
keep your elbows off the table
ever since i've turned 50 or so
are we that way with our own offspring
of course we are different
let them write about us
over time

April 2018

风景

楼梯间里

小窗的

风景

仿佛照相机。

有点凉意。

这张照片很壮丽，

可你只感觉到穿堂而过的风。

你不能随身带走它

无论你去向哪里，

可你为什么要这么做

2018.4

THE VIEW

the view

from the little window

in the staircase

is like a camera.

it’s a little cold.

the picture is magnificent,

but you feel the draft.

you can’t take it with you

wherever you’ll go,

but why would you want to

April 2018

玛丽亚

玛丽亚真的很少女

至少在某次顶礼膜拜中

在里皮给她加冕的典礼上

十四五岁的样子

那便是为什么整个故事如此荒谬

如此纯洁，如此神圣

她压根儿不知道发生了什么。

2018.4

MARIA

maria is really very young

at least in the one adoration

and in her coronation by lippi

14, 15

that's why the whole story is so preposterous

and so pure and so holy

she doesn't know what happened at all.

April 2018

来自佛罗伦萨

来自佛罗伦萨的葡萄酒味道很好。
并非名酒
只是来自有机农贸市场
在圣神大殿前
无标签
但就像整个城市整个省一样真实
该省
很有泥土气
虽然可以
论证
现代性就来自该城
我想知道他们是否
在犹太礼拜中使用葡萄酒
我敢肯定在犹太教堂
石壁上铭刻的
那场盛大的婚礼中
他们有酒
最近的一个婚礼
来自英格兰的两个人

他们肯定也举行的是当地婚礼
完全执行所有礼节的一座犹太教堂
高大美丽的独立式穹顶
没有米兰大教堂那么大
但却傲立可见
从远处
摩尔人的风格，
也可能是拜占庭
你可以说
在十九世纪
基督徒的推算中
在户外
建造如此巨大的上帝之家
是安全的
这是解放的
时代
现代性失败
基督教失败
于阻止一切
虽然有些是隐藏的
虽然有些幸存下来
欧洲的大多数犹太教堂消失了

宗教讨论
无神论什么的
而不是人类的未来
全都毫无意义
这便是我们来的地方
如果我们拥有任何一种
这栋楼
这座城市
这片土地
这种酒
如果我们现在有
或过去有任何一种
这种农夫的酒
这片农村
这座城市
在许多其他事物中间
就是我们要去的地方
你不需要机器
或者几乎不要任何
这样的历史
你不需要电脑
不是真的

如果已经有

如果我们可以有

就在这里。

干杯！

2018.4

FROM FLORENCE

the wine from florence tastes very good
not a famous wine
just from the organic farmers' market
in front of santo spirito
no label
but just as real as the whole town
and the province
earthy
although this is the city
where modernity comes from
arguably
i wonder if they use wine
in jewish services
i'm pretty sure they had wine
at the big wedding
commemorated in stone
at the synagogue
a recent wedding
two people from england

they must have local weddings too

a synagogue in full working order

big beautiful free-standing dome

not as big as the duomo

but standing proud to be seen

from afar

moorish style,

byzantine probably

you could say

in the 19th century

of christian reckoning

it was thought to be safe

to build such a large house of god

in the open

it was the age

of emancipation

modernity failed

christianity failed

to prevent anything

although some were hidden

although some survived

most synagogues in europe are gone

discussing religion
atheism whatever
the future of mankind not
is all very idle
this is where we come from
if there is any we
this building
this city
this country
this wine
if there is
or was any we
this farmer's wine
this countryside
this city
among many others
is where we are going
you don't need machines
or hardly any
for this kind of history
you don't need computers
not really

if there has been

if there can be any we

it is here.

cheers!

April 2018

空教堂

坐在空荡荡的教堂里很好。

你在这里不重要，

你的生命不重要。

就像当你爬到山脊的时候，

你看到远方的山峰，

和山谷之间。

你可以看到整个山谷。

不知怎的，这次你看得更加清楚，在这个空荡荡的教堂里。

这意味着你虔信吗

有一次你爬到屋顶上。

这是一座大教堂，你可以看到很远。

你和朋友们爬上去，和你的家人在一起。

有一轮满月。

你们拥有一个美好的时刻，你们所有人。

他们一年只玩一次，甚至更少。

让人们爬到那里。

这是一个大圆顶。

坐在空荡荡的教堂里很好。

它并非真的空荡荡，

人们有时在里面走来走去。
如果它是空的，
它会被锁上。
不管怎样，它足够大了，
没人打扰你。
你坚信你可以写完一首诗。

2018.6

EMPTY CHURCH

it's good to sit in an empty church.
you don't matter here,
your life doesn't matter.
it's like when you're up on a ridge,
you see the mountains far in the distance,
and the valley between.
you can see the whole valley.
somehow this time you see it more clearly in this empty church.
does this mean you believe
one time you were up on the roof.
it's a big church, you can see very far.
you were up there with friends, and with your family.
it was a full moon.
you had a great time, all of you.
they do this only once in a year, or even less often.
to let people up there.
it's a big dome.
it's good to sit in an empty church.

it’s not really empty,

people walk back and forth once in a while.

if it was empty,

it would be locked.

anyway, it’s big enough,

nobody bothers you.

you believe you can finish a poem.

June 2018

有时[1]

有时你能够回到过去。
你走回一幢房子，
你走回一片海滩，
你回去采蓝莓。
你经常能够发现许多其他小浆果，
在苏联时代遗留下的房子后面。
他们经常从那座房子窥视全城。
不高，很长。
变成了游览胜地。
那座房子现在消失了，
希望他们没动那片森林。
有时你能够回到过去。
树枝摇曳，
和风吹拂，
几乎与祖母的时代没有两样。
我能肯定的只是落日依旧美丽
经过战争、屠杀与放逐。

---

1 作者写的是拉脱维亚，其岳父是拉脱维亚人，后移居美国，现居德国。——译注

有时你能够回到过去。
祖母的房子还在，
你唱着祖母时代的歌
在大舞台上和成千上万的人一起。
你叔叔的遗孀还在，
那里总会有你的亲戚。
有时你能够回到过去。
五年前，我们在这里
之前也来过，
当时孩子们还很小
适合自行车驮运。
我们骑着租来的自行车穿过森林
到达半岛的顶端。
这里非常美丽，
希望他们保护好它。
房子大概是 1970 年代建的，
其他历史的记忆
包括 1990 年。
独立，
你的遗产的重新发现。
一个不稳定的未来。
有时你能够
回到过去。

2018.7

SOMETIMES

sometimes you can go back in time.
you go back to a house,
you go back to a beach,
you go back to pick blueberries.
you used to find many other small berries,
behind the house left from soviet times.
they used to spy on the whole town from that house.
not tall, rather long,
converted for tourists.
that house is gone now,
hope they left the woods alone.
sometimes you can go back in time.
trees would have swayed,
wind would have blown
almost the same in grandmother's time.
i'm sure the sunset was just as beautiful
through war and holocaust and deportation.
sometimes you can go back in time.
grandmother's house is here,

you sang the songs from grandmother's time
on the big stage with thousands and thousands.
zile is here,
your relatives will always be here.
sometimes you can go back in time.
we were here five years ago
and before,
when the kids were small
and fit in a bicycle carrier.
we rode rented bikes and walked through the woods
to the tip of the peninsula.
very nice there,
hope they preserve it.
housing from the 70s maybe,
other historical memories
including 1990.
independence,
rediscovery of your inheritance.
a precarious future.
sometimes you can
go back in time.

July 2018

日落

每次我看到日落
我都问自己人们在等待什么
不，不是真的
人们只是在那儿观看日落
闻闻草，感受风
听听蟋蟀，听听这个城市，
这座建筑，空气流动的声音。
看看阴影
站在屋顶
等待夜晚
写一首诗

2018.8

SUNSET

every time i watch the sunset
i ask myself what people are for
no, not really
people are there to watch the sunset
to smell the grass, to feel the wind
to hear the crickets, the city,
this building, the ventilation.
to see the shadows
to stand on a roof
to wait for the night
and write a poem

August 2018

马略卡 1

马略卡感觉像台湾

让我想家

在凌晨一点

某种香味，也许是茉莉花

雨

我们在一场暴雨中到达

第二天多雨

疲倦

天空并不阴暗，但却在下雨

现在有阳光

只是一点点

而且仍然下雨

然后它停了一会儿

几乎

2018.10

MAJORCA 1

majorca feels like taiwan
makes me homesick
at one in the morning
some kind of scent, maybe jasmine
rain
we arrive in a rainstorm
lots of rain next day
tired
sky isn't dark but it rains
and now there is sun
just a little
and it still rains
then it stops for a while
almost

October 2018

马略卡 2

初雪降临
在山中的某个地方
才十月
我们在《德意志岛屿新闻》上听到的
在一家超市里
还有一棵树倒在某个地方
造成一些损失
超市的一半都是葡萄酒区
瓶子之间有海盗雕像
罗马遗址占据最好的时间点
当地文化在公元前 600 年左右达到高峰
然后罗马人来了
然后基思 · 理查兹来了
以及迭戈 · 马拉多纳
其间不能忘记阿拉伯人也来了
我们在同一个地方吃比萨
真好
在基思还是罗恩 · 伍德之后
其他人都来了

在我们的公寓里

wifi 仍然不能用

空调供暖

让我头痛

外面的空气一定好极了

今天两个女孩在楼下的游泳池里游泳

也许雨停了五分钟

人们在阿尔库迪亚港

的海滩游泳

有一个救生员

穿着一件雨衣

那是一座美丽的岛屿

2018.10

MAJORCA 2

first snow has fallen
somewhere in the mountains
it's still october
we hear it on *german island news*
in a supermarket
also a tree has fallen somewhere
and caused some damage
half of the supermarket is wine
a pirate statue among the bottles
the roman ruins have a good timeline
local culture peaked around 600 bc
then came the romans
then came keith richards
and diego maradona
in between came the arabs not to forget
we ate pizza at the same place
it was really good
after keith or was it ron wood
came everyone else

wifi still doesn’t work

in our apartment

the air-condition-heating

gives me a headache

the air outside must still be wonderful

two girls swam in the pool downstairs today

maybe the rain stopped for 5 minutes

people swam at the beach

of port alcudia

there was a lifeguard

in a raincoat

it’s a beautiful island

October 2018

马略卡 3

只有一点点阳光
下午
在最后一日
昨天我们爬了当地的小山
希望山羊没事
一只小山羊滑倒了
逃离我们
站起来没问题，它妈妈在等着
我发现了一个鸟类保护区
就在当地大超市旁边
玛雅在南瓜上雕刻
杰基做了一顿丰盛的晚餐
我们玩得开心，我们四个
到晚上我病了
到早上
利奥也病了，现在他好了
我们在宾馆里
大家都说雨太大了
至少不像在东方

有人死于洪水
在这儿很正常，我想
或多或少
我们得收拾行李了
明天一早天不亮
就要离开

2018.10

MAJORCA 3

just a little bit of sun
in the afternoon
on our last day
yesterday we climbed the local hill
hope the goats are ok
a little goat slipped and fell
running from us
got up no problem, mama was waiting
i discovered a bird sanctuary
right next to the big local supermarket
maia carved a pumpkin
jackie cooked a good dinner
we had fun, the four of us
i was sick in the night
and in the morning
leo too, now he's fine
we are in the hotel
everyone says the rain is too much
at least it's not like in the east

people died from the floods

here it's normal i guess

more or less

we have to pack

and leave early tomorrow

when it's still dark

October 2018

好音乐会

每一场好音乐会
会把你带向
很远很远的远方
从一座城市
到另一座
从维也纳
到维也纳
一个没有内政部长
的维也纳
任何内政部长
不论男的还是女的
过去三十年间
也许曾短暂地
有过
一个正派的人
他是作曲家
之子。
每一场好音乐会
会把你带向

很远很远的远方
这就是为什么
有如此之多的
好音乐会
在维也纳。

2018.11

GOOD CONCERT

every good concert
carries you
far far away
from one city
to another
from vienna
to vienna
a vienna without
an interior minister.
any interior minister
male or female
last thirty years
maybe there was
one decent person
for a short time
he was the son
of a composer.
every good concert
carries you

far far away

this is why

there are so many

good concerts

in vienna.

November 2018

没有什么

没有什么比晨曦更好
没有什么比夜阑更好
还有黑暗
还有寂静

没有什么比拥抱你更好
总是这样

没有什么比相拥更好
没有什么只是没有什么
比光更轻

2018.12

NOTHING

there is nothing better than light in the morning
there is nothing better than light in the night
and darkness
and quiet

there is nothing better than to hold you
always

nothing better than holding each other
nothing but nothing
is lighter than light

December 2018

手机

我想我已经拥有它七年了。

四年前跟伊沙在佛蒙特时已有。

四年半，感觉像永远。

是 LG，韩国品牌吗

当然是中国制造的，从未查过。

无法拍照，镜头被刮伤了。

否则就完美了，

微信也能用，

让我用了这么久。

感觉我在中国时也用过，

2008 年和那之前。

但我知道智能手机是新生事物

十年前，或是九年前才出现。

爸爸，你是什么时候拿到你的第一台手机的

在你 2002 年出生的时候。

妈妈先有了一台，当然是诺基亚。

有一阵子我们俩共用这一台。

那张斯芬克斯的照片，你站在阴影中，

用在我个人资料中的那张，

是我用一个更原始的手机拍的，
比这个更原始。
但阳光正好。

2019.1

PHONE

think i've had it for seven years.
had it in vermont four years ago with yisha.
four and a half years, feels like forever.
it's lg, is that korean
made in china of course, never checked.
can't take photos, lens is all scratched.
otherwise it's fine,
even wechat works,
far as i use it.
feels like i've had it in china,
2008 and before.
but i know smartphones were new
ten years ago, or even nine.
daddy, when did you get your first mobile phone
when you were born, in 2002.
mami had one first, of course a nokia.
for a while we used one between the two of us.
that photograph of the sphinx, where you're in the shadow,
the one from my profile,

i took it with a more primitive phone,

much more primitive than this one.

but the sun was just right.

January 2019

我们

我们不是明亮的光，
只是一点微弱的反射
在大海深处的某个地方。
当我们能够看到珊瑚
听到来自高远天空
的声音时。
我们害怕
我们自己的影子。

2019.2

WE

we are no bright light,
just a feeble reflection
somewhere down in the ocean.
when we can, we see the corals
and hear the sound
high up in the sky.
we're afraid
of our own shadow.

February 2019

时间

我写诗的最佳时间
是在我有时间的时候，
当我拥有这个世界上所有的时间
并且毫不在意。
我有足够的时间阅读
余华的每一部长篇小说和许多短篇小说，
只因喜欢他的语言感觉
阅读莫言的《酒国》
全是中文。
我写诗不多。
玛雅还小。她出生前我有的是时间。
其实，还是诗歌翻译做得更多
在乐友出生前就开始了。
不管怎样，我们在中国
永远。

2019.6

TIME

my best time for writing poetry
was when i had time,
when i had all the time in the world
and nary a care.
i had time enough to read
yu hua's every novel and many stories,
just because of the feel of his language
and *republic of wine* by mo yan
all in chinese.
i didn't write many poems.
maia was small. i had time before her.
actually, translating more poetry
began just before leo was born.
anyway, we were in china
forever.

June 2019

译后记

文 | 伊沙

我的大学时代正值20世纪80年代中后期，上进青年一致向西看，顶礼膜拜西方大师，我在我的同学中还不算最严重的，当时我说了这样一句话：我更关心西方国家里我的同辈人、同龄人在写什么以及如何写。

毕业不久，我把这句话写进了文章。

中国有句厉害的谚语："不怕贼偷，就怕贼惦记"——凭我的经验，但凡正念，就有可能被惦记。2013年冬，在我说出那句话的25年以后，一位与我同龄（小我不到一个月）的奥地利诗人，空降西安来到我面前。他的中文名字叫维马丁，此前他是以翻译家的身份与我通信的，他去台湾访问时读到了我的诗集《尿床》，有兴趣将我的诗整本地译成德语并在德语国家出版。此次他专程到访西安，也主要是为了这件事。也许是出于诗人本色吧，他在给我看德语杂志上他译的中国诗人（包括我在内）的诗作的同时，也给我看了他发表在杂志上的自己的几首诗。那一年前后我和老G正在狂译世界各国诗人的作品，回家后我见他的诗有英语版，顺手就译了，次日见面拿给他看，他非常高兴，也十分欣赏我的译笔。

对维马丁作品的翻译便从这时开始了，但也并未马上进入日常状态，总是见一次面翻译几首。2014 年秋，我们一起得到了美国亨利·鲁斯基金会创设的“中文诗歌创作与翻译奖金”，共享在佛蒙特创作中心驻留写作翻译一个月的奖励——那是我生命中最幸福的时光之一；2015 年春，在维马丁的大力举荐下，我应奥地利两校一刊的邀请访问了他高雅的祖国；2015 年夏，我们相会于“青海湖国际诗歌节”，又转道西安去了“《新世纪诗典》·崆峒山诗会”，在这次诗会上我向他颁发了“NPC李白诗歌奖”首设的翻译奖；2016 年，他应邀加入《新世纪诗典》诗人新马泰访问团，并获得那次国际诗会的总冠军。通过这几次对其诗作的翻译，我已经很有把握地判断出：这是一位真正的诗人，也是一位优秀的诗人。我暗自决定要专辟时间，将其诗作整本地翻译出来。

总是很忙，工作安排得很满，等到把时间专辟出来，已经到了去年下半年，我和老 G 用了一个学期加半个寒假的时间，终于将本书译成了。

每译一组，我心中维马丁的诗人形象都要高大一分，那么他究竟是多大的一位诗人？中国人喜欢终极评价，身为译者你不做出这样的评价，自己心里都发虚。

作为翻译家的维马丁，似乎在中国的官方和民间诗坛都有很高的评价。他获得了《人民文学》杂志2018年度奖的翻译奖，并且他早就被聘为《人民文学》德语版《路灯》的主编；在民间的《新世纪诗典》这边，他译有大量中国诗人的诗作并在德语国家发表，《新世纪诗典》德语版也即将在奥地利出版，他翻译的我的诗集《车过黄河1》《车过黄河2》都已在奥地利出版。

那么，作为诗人的他，究竟是多大的诗人？

我听到最高的评价是来自西方文学修养深厚的中国诗人、诗评家徐江，他称其为“一位大师，欧洲在世者中最优秀的诗人”。

作为译者，我的评价较为谨慎，面向本书：这是目前在世的外国诗人在中国出版的最耐读、最优秀的一部诗集。

但是且慢，我还要提醒大家：我和老G只懂英语不懂德语，我们是通过英译本转译的，德语——他母语中的维马丁才是百分百的维马丁。好在我们的翻译善于美化原作者（由于中文功底深厚），翻译的过程中，我和他也时有细致的讨论，多少能把从德语到英语的损失弥补了吧。事实上，维马丁既有直接用英文写的诗，又有直接用中文写的诗，能够掌握八种语言的他，是个语言的奇才。

请你们——本书的所有读者，用中文版评估：维马丁究竟是多大的诗人？

奥地利文化部有一项政策：翻译奥地利作家的作品，可以获邀赴奥住上一段时间。我们的申请批下来时，本书已经译完了，我也快开学了，不宜动身，那就等译下一本的时候吧。在我这里，维马丁将享有与伟大的布考斯基同等的待遇：终生译。

2019 年 2 月 16 于西安少陵塬

AFTERWORD

by Yi Sha

My college time fell exactly into the end of the 1980s. Progressive young people were altogether looking westwards, taking off their hats to Western grand masters. I was not as forward in this respect as some of my fellow students. Back then I said this: "I am more interested in what and how my contemporaries are writing in Western countries."

Not long after I graduated, I wrote this sentence into an essay.

We have a saying in Chinese: "I am not afraid of a thief stealing, but of a thief keeping something in mind" — in my experience, anything that I am conscious of can finally succeed. In the winter of 2013, a poet from Austria who is exactly my age (3 weeks younger) came to my old Xi'an out of the blue. His Chinese name is Wei Mading. He had contacted me before as a translator, and he had encountered my poetry in Taiwan, a book called *Wetting the Bed*. He was interested in my poetry as a whole, hoping to translate it into German and publish it in German-speaking countries. This was the reason why he came here to meet me. He showed me newspapers and magazines with Chinese poetry translated into German, including his translations of my poems. At the same time he also showed me some of his own poetry, being published in the same places. Old G and I were right in the middle of translating a lot of poetry from all over the world, so once we realized he had poems in English, we translated a few. When Martin saw them, he was very happy, and also very appreciative of how his poems came out in our versions.

This is how it began. At first, it wasn't a daily affair, but just a few poems each time we met. In the fall of 2014, we were both awarded a Henry Luce Chinese Poetry Fellowship at Vermont Studio Center, so we were able to write and translate in America for a whole month—one of the happiest times I ever had. In the spring of 2015, through Martin's ardent recommendation, two universities and one magazine together invited me to visit his exalted home country. In the summer of 2015, we met at Qinghai International Poetry Festival, and went on together to the *NPC* Poetry Festival at Kongtong Mountain. At the latter festival, I awarded him the Li Bai Poetry Prize for Translation. In 2016, he was invited to our *NPC* poetry journey to Singapore, Malaysia and Thailand, and came out first in the accompanying poetry competitions. Through these encounters, I gradually received a thoroughly informed opinion: This is a real poet, an outstanding poet. I resolved to myself to find the time to translate a whole book of his poetry.

But I was always very busy, and I hadn't really found time until last year. It took Old G and me one semester and half of our winter holiday to finish translating his poetry.

With every set of poetry I translated, my image of Martin as a poet went up another measure. So how great is he after all? Chinese people like to talk in superlatives, and as his translator, if I don't do this, I will feel uneasy.

As a translator, he is obviously respected both in official and non-official poetry circles in China. Right around the New Year of 2018, he won the *People's Literature* Translation Prize, and he has been chief editor for the German version of this flagship literary magazine since the beginning of 2015. On the non-official side, he has published many translations of *NPC* poets in German-speaking countries, as well as two books of my poems, and more books are coming out as *NPC* anthologies.

But as a poet, how great is he?

The highest appreciation I have heard comes from the poet and critic Xu Jiang, who steeps in Western literary theory. He calls Martin the most outstanding European poet alive.

As a translator, I have to be somewhat cautious, but I can say: This is the most enjoyable book in China by a living foreign poet.

And there is one more thing: Old G and I translated from English because we don't read German. German is his mother tongue, so he must be even more in his element there. Even though we improved the literary flavor in the target language here and there, this would only make up for what was lost in the English versions versus the German ones. Actually, Martin also writes directly in English and Chinese. He speaks many tongues; language is his main talent.

Please tell me, after you read the Chinese versions here: How great is this poet?

The Austrian Ministry of Culture has a program to

invite translators of Austrian literature to Austria. We didn't realize this in time for this book, but let us do it for the next one. I have resolved to treat Martin Winter like I treat the great Charles Bukowski: I will translate him as long as I live.

02/16/2019, Shaolingyuan, Xi'an

图书在版编目（CIP）数据

最终我们赢得了雪：维马丁诗选：汉英对照 /（奥）维马丁著；伊沙，老G译. — 成都：四川文艺出版社，2020.9
ISBN 978-7-5411-5724-0

Ⅰ. ①最… Ⅱ. ①维… ②伊… ③老… Ⅲ. ①英语—汉语—对照读物②诗集—奥地利—现代 Ⅳ. ①H319.4：I

中国版本图书馆CIP数据核字（2020）第141063号

著作权合同登记号　图进字：21-2020-266

ZUIZHONG WOMEN YING DE LE XUE WEIMADING SHIXUAN

最终我们赢得了雪：维马丁诗选

【奥地利】维马丁　著　伊沙　老G　译

出 品 人　张庆宁
责任编辑　李　博
特约监制　里　所
特约编辑　修宏烨
封面设计　周伟伟
责任校对　汪　平

出版发行　四川文艺出版社（成都市槐树街2号）
网　　址　www.scwys.com
电　　话　028-86259287（发行部）　028-86259303（编辑部）
传　　真　028-86259306

邮购地址　成都市槐树街2号四川文艺出版社邮购部　610031
印　　刷　河北鹏润印刷有限公司
成品尺寸　130mm × 198mm　　开　　本　32开
印　　张　8.25　　字　　数　165千
版　　次　2020年9月第一版　　印　　次　2020年9月第一次印刷
书　　号　ISBN 978-7-5411-5724-0
定　　价　78.00元

磨铁诗歌译丛

已出版

磨 铁 读 诗 会